IMAGES
of Sports

THE AMERICAN LEAGUE
THE EARLY YEARS

The Founder of the American League. Byron Bancroft Johnson quit his job as sports editor of the Cincinnati *Commercial-Gazette* in 1894 to take over an almost defunct Western League as president. A hot-tempered, stubborn, uncompromising man, Johnson found the men to bankroll his teams, came down hard on rowdy behavior and roughhousing on the field, and enforced respect for umpires. By 1900, the best-run circuit in baseball had changed its name to the American League and had challenged the National League for major league status. In 1903, the National League was forced to agree to parity with the junior circuit.

IMAGES
of Sports

THE AMERICAN LEAGUE
THE EARLY YEARS

David Lee Poremba

ARCADIA
PUBLISHING

Published by Arcadia Publishing
Charleston, South Carolina

Library of Congress Catalog Card Number: 00-103958

For all general information contact Arcadia Publishing at:
Telephone 843-853-2070
Fax 843-853-0044
E-Mail sales@arcadiapublishing.com
For customer service and orders:
Toll-Free 1-888-313-2665

Visit us on the Internet at www.arcadiapublishing.com

The Dead-Ball Era. The new American League gave baseball fans a cleaner brand of ball. President Johnson successfully combated bad manners and the offensive extremes of rowdy ball. As the players settled down and put their minds to the game, they found it was scientific and soaked in strategy. Scores were kept necessarily low, and rarely were league home run champions in double digits.

CONTENTS

ACKNOWLEDGMENTS

As always, the Ernie Harwell Sports Collection at the Burton Historical Collection, Detroit Public Library continues to provide unmatched examples of period photographs of our National Pastime.

The author is grateful for the use of the cover photograph, which comes from the Richard Bak Collection.

There are numbers of useful and entertaining reference materials on baseball available at libraries everywhere. The two most useful in this project were: *The Ballplayers: Baseball's Ultimate Biographical Reference*, and, *The Baseball Encyclopedia, 6th Edition.*

I would be remiss without acknowledging the continued support of my lovely wife, Kate.

INTRODUCTION

The American League was founded nearly a century ago when Western League President Ban Johnson renamed the circuit in 1900 and declared the American a major league in 1901. Johnson had made the Western League the strongest minor league during the late 1890s. Taking advantage of a National League struggle to name a president and the expiration of the National Agreement that governed the baseball world, Johnson went into open competition for players and fans. The St. Paul club was moved from Minnesota to Chicago, and the League met the Nationals head on in Boston and Philadelphia, too. The other franchises were located in Detroit, Milwaukee, Cleveland, Baltimore, and Washington D.C. The National League owners were leaderless and, having just gone from twelve teams to eight, were in no position to prevent this. The war was on.

Ignoring the reserve clause in National League contracts, which tied players to one team for life, Ban Johnson stocked his new league with major league players by offering higher salaries. National League clubs enforced a salary maximum of $2,400 for their players, making it easier to lure stars such as Cy Young, John McGraw, Willie Keeler, Napoleon Lajoie, Ed Delahanty, and others away. Connie Mack, the manager of the Philadelphia Athletics, signed Lajoie by offering him a $6,000 contract. Over 100 National League players jumped to the American League.

The junior circuit, backed by solidarity and the insistence of fair, clean play, outdrew the National League in attendance. Johnson insisted on presenting to the paying public a better brand of baseball. He denounced rowdy behavior and drunkenness on and off the field and strongly supported his umpires' decisions. In 1902, he moved the Milwaukee club to St. Louis, and now directly competing in four cities, once again outdrew the National League; overall attendance for the eight-team league was 2,228,000 over a 136-game schedule, compared to 1,684,000 for the National League.

After the 1902 season, the National League owners favored a return to the dual major league structure similar to the one they had with the American Association during the 1880s. The National Agreement of 1903 stated that both circuits were separate but equal major leagues, had common playing rules, mutually accommodating schedules, and recognized each league's territories and player contracts. This last stipulation restored the reserve clause to the detriment of the players. The American League got to keep all of the players who jumped, was allowed to move the Baltimore club to New York, and agreed not to place a franchise in Pittsburgh (which would have been the Detroit club). The Agreement set up a three-member National Commission to govern the game. The three members were the National League President Harry Pulliam, Ban Johnson, and Cincinnati Reds owner Garry Hermann.

Peace prevailed in baseball. Buoyed by rising attendance and increased media coverage, no franchise changes occurred over the next 50 years. Attendance rose from 4.7 million in 1903 to 10 million in 1911. The prosperity spurred the construction, from 1909 to 1911, of new steel and concrete stadiums large enough to hold all these new fans.

The game of baseball was one of strategy, centered on bunts, hit-and-run tactics, and base stealing. The game was more scientific, and every run counted for much. Boston, Philadelphia, Chicago, and Detroit dominated the pennant races during the first two decades of the league's existence. Each year the pennant races were tight, being decided in the last month of the season.

In 1910, the cork-centered baseball was introduced and the game became livelier. Babe Ruth came on the scene and introduced a whole new style of play with the home run. Starting in 1920, the game would change forever.

Here in these photographs are the managers and players of the eight-team league that shed its regionalism and called itself American. There are superstars, journeymen ballplayers, and those men of even lesser talents pictured here in all the glory of their time.

One

A LEAGUE IS FORMED

Magnates of the Western League, 1899. Ban Johnson sits (third from the left) surrounded by the owners of the franchises of the soon-to-be American League. From left to right, they are as follows: (front row) T.J. Lofters, Louisville; M.J. O'Brien; Ban Johnson, President; J.H. Manning, Kansas City; George A. VanderBeck, Detroit; and C.H. Snurlpaugh, Minneapolis; (back row) R. Allen, Indianapolis; M.R. Killilea, Milwaukee; Connie Mack, Milwaukee; Charles A. Comisky, St. Paul; and G.H. Schmelz. After making the Western the strongest league in the country, Johnson was ready to challenge the National League for major-league status. In 1900, the National League dropped several teams, and Johnson made his move. Shifting the St. Paul club to Chicago and putting a club into the vacated city of Cleveland, the league opened the 1900 season with eight teams in Buffalo, Chicago, Cleveland, Detroit, Indianapolis, Kansas City, Milwaukee, and Minneapolis. To ensure solidarity amongst the scattered teams, Johnson renamed it the American League. Chicago won the inaugural flag by four and one-half games.

The 1900 Detroit Club. This edition of the charter Detroit team finished fourth in 1900, twelve-and-a-half games off the mark. It was on the road that they went flat with a 24-42 showing. Pitcher Jack Cronin led the league in complete games with 36, and strikeouts with 121.

Sam Crawford, 1903. Properly attired with his hair slicked back and jersey buttoned up, 23-year-old Crawford poses for the first time as a Tiger. Born in Wahoo, Nebraska, Sam gave up barbering and started with the Cincinnati Reds in 1899. He hit a then-astonishing total of 16 home runs in 1901 to lead the National League.

George Barclay Mercer. A right-handed pitcher, Win Mercer led the National League Washington club, going 25-18 in 1896 and 20-20 in 1897. He joined the Tigers in 1902 and posted a career-best 3.02 earned run average. When not pitching he often played the outfield, as well as some infield. The Tigers appointed the 28-year-old their player manager for 1903, but that January Win Mercer committed suicide in a San Francisco hotel by inhaling poison gas.

The First American League Champions, 1901. Owner Charles Comisky stands out amidst his Chicago White Stockings in this group pose. Seated to his left is pitcher and manager Clark Griffith (13), who posted a 24-7 record while jockeying the club to a 83-53 mark, 4 games ahead of second-place Boston. The team scored a league leading 819 runs while the pitching staff posted a stingy 2.98 ERA.

William Ellsworth Hoy. Pictured here as a center fielder for Washington in his rookie year of 1888, "Dummy" Hoy finished his major league career with Chicago in 1901, batting sixth with a .294 average. The reason umpires adopted hand signals to go along with the "strike," "out," and "safe" calls was to accommodate Hoy, who was a deaf-mute. The 5-foot, 4-inch outfielder accumulated over 2,000 hits in his career and led the league in putouts and total chances.

Lafayette Napoleon Cross. Lave Cross was another National Leaguer who switched over to the American in 1901. The bow-legged third baseman played in 447 consecutive games from 1902 to 1905 and for seven straight seasons (1898–1904), and he never batted below .290. Enjoying a 21-year career in four major leagues, Cross played for Connie Mack's Philadelphia A's before finishing his last two seasons with Washington (1906–07).

Ed Siever. This 6-foot left-hander broke into the majors with Detroit in 1901, completing 30 of 33 games for an 18-15 record. In 1902, he led the American League with a 1.91 ERA, but went 8-11. Sold to the St. Louis Browns after the 1902 season, he went 13-14 and 10-15 with them before being released. Out of baseball in 1905, he got another chance with the Tigers in 1906 and helped them to win their first pennant in 1907.

James R. McAleer. Jimmy McAleer spent ten seasons as an outfielder with the Cleveland Spiders and retired in 1898. He came out of retirement to manage the St. Louis Browns in 1902 and continued there for eight seasons, finishing second that first season, which would be his best record. Jimmy moved on to Washington for two seasons in 1910 before becoming part owner of the Boston Red Sox in 1912.

Napoleon Lajoie. "Larry" Lajoie joined the Philadelphia Phillies for the 1896 season and played first base in 39 games. He became a regular the next season and hit .363, leading the National League in slugging percentage. In 1898, the Rhode Island native moved to second base and topped the league in RBIs with 127 and doubles with 40. He is considered the greatest second baseman in baseball history. In 1901, he jumped across town to Connie Mack's Athletics, helping to give the new circuit some credibility. He led the new league in several categories, and his .422 batting average still stands as the league record. The following year the Phillies obtained a court injunction forbidding him from playing in Pennsylvania. As a hedge against unpredictable court proceedings, Ban Johnson transferred his contract to Cleveland, where his arrival invigorated a listless franchise. He became a popular player with both fans and teammates.

The 1902 Cleveland Blues. Dressed in their blue uniforms, the Blues changed their name to the Bronchos; upon the acquisition of Nap Lajoie, they became the Naps. Led by William Armour (in bowler hat), the Naps finished in fifth place despite Lajoie's .366 batting average, good for second place among the league leaders. First baseman "Piano Legs" Hickman hit .363, with 11 home runs. Rookie pitcher Addie Joss posted a 17-13 record.

Red Donahue, 1903. Newly acquired from the St. Louis Browns in mid-season, Francis Rostell Donahue was a veteran National League pitcher, brought in to bolster Cleveland's staff. He would enjoy his best season in the American League in 1904, posting a 19-14 record and a 2.40 ERA. Red completed 30 of 33 games started and struck out 127 batters.

15

The Franchise Player. One of the most powerful and consistent hitters of the dead-ball era, Larry Lajoie was the reason baseball survived along the shores of Lake Erie. Setting the league batting mark with a .422 average in 1901, he led the circuit twice more, hitting .355 in 1903 and .381 in 1904. A right-handed pull hitter, his 648 lifetime doubles ranks him tenth all-time.

William "Kid" Gleason. Another veteran National Leaguer who jumped to the AL in 1901, Gleason earned his nickname partly because of his 5-foot, 9-inch height and mostly because of his enthusiasm. He began his career with the Phillies in 1888 and blossomed into a star right-hander. When the pitching distance was increased in 1894, he lost his effectiveness and switched to second base. Joining the Tigers for two seasons, he returned to the Phillies for four more seasons before moving into the coaching ranks.

James Barrett. A Massachusetts native, Jimmy joined the Detroit club in 1901 after two seasons with Cincinnati. He hit a solid .293 that year followed by two .300 seasons, leading the league in walks in 1903 and 1904. A sturdy outfielder with an exceptional throwing arm, Barrett led the American League in assists in three of the first four seasons of the circuit. His career was ended prematurely by a knee injury.

George Edward Waddell. No one need look any further to define the word eccentric than to Rube Waddell, who held up the start of games he was scheduled to pitch while he played marbles with children outside the park. Waddell signed his first contract with Louisville in 1897. He jumped the Pittsburgh team because he was unhappy with the stern discipline of manager Fred Clarke. Connie Mack signed him for his Milwaukee club in 1900 and went 24-7 for Mack's 1902 Athletics.

"Gettysburg" Eddie Plank. A graduate of Gettysburg College, Eddie was signed as a rather elderly rookie of 25 by the Athletics in 1901 and became the major left-hander of the great Philadelphia teams. He had excellent control and was a deliberate pitcher, going 17-13 in his rookie year. He would post twenty-plus win seasons in five of the next six seasons.

Early Action, 1903. In what is probably the first action-sports picture taken, New York Highlander third baseman Wid Conroy leaps high into the air to haul down an errant outfield throw while an unidentified Detroit Tiger makes to slide headfirst into the bag. Umpire "Silk" O'Laughlin (right) is in position to make the call.

Ready At The Plate. William Edward Conroy stands in against opposition pitching in 1903, his first year in the American League. He picked up the nickname "Widow" for his concern for younger boys on sandlot teams and was known as "Wid" throughout the rest of his career. He led the AL twice in total chances per game.

"Happy Jack" Chesbro. Jack Chesbro worked his way through the minor leagues and finally joined the Pittsburgh Pirates in mid-season 1899. He pitched the Pirates to their first pennants in 1901 and 1902, going 21-10 and 28-6 respectively. He picked up the spitball in 1902, which helped to prolong his relatively short career. Joining the Highlanders in 1903, he chalked up an incredible 41 wins in 1904, pitching 454 innings in 55 games.

Walter Clarkson. Youngest of three pitching Clarkson brothers, Walter pitched for Harvard when the Ivy League School dominated college baseball. His brothers' Dad (Arthur) and John both pitched in the NL in the 1880's and 1890's. Signing with New York in 1904, Walter enjoyed his best season in 1906, going 9-4 with an ERA of 2.32.

Hit 'Em Where They Ain't. "Wee Willie" Keeler was an established star when he jumped to the New York Highlanders in 1903. Starting out with the New York Giants in 1892, Keeler came into his own as the lead-off batter for the World Champion Baltimore Orioles from 1894 to 1898. Moving to Brooklyn after the Orioles were broken up, Keeler maintained his excellent bat control, becoming a precise bunter and place hitter. He is one of the few players to play for all three New York teams.

Denton True Young. Judged to be "as fast as a cyclone," Cy Young had amassed 285 victories in an 11 year NL career before jumping to the Boston Red Sox in 1901. He led the league in victories the first three years of the American League's existence. Cy went 2-1 in the very first World Series in 1903 with a 1.59 ERA. The 6-foot, 2-inch, 210-pound right-hander, pictured here at spring training in Arkansas, has a career victory total of 511, just about split evenly between the two leagues. His 22 seasons spans the early history of the game from a pitching distance of 50-feet to the present 60-feet, 6-inches; he pitched against Cap Anson, an established NL star when that league was formed in 1876, and against Eddie Collins, who played into the 1930's. He pitched until he was 44 years old, when portliness, not arm trouble, suggested his retirement.

Charles Sylvester Stahl. "Chick" Stahl broke into the major leagues with the NL Boston Beaneaters in 1897, batting .358 with 13 triples. He topped the .300 mark in five of his first six seasons. Chick moved to the Boston Americans in 1901 and continued his fine play. In 1903, he hit 3 triples in the World Series and led the AL with 19 in 1904. He became the Red Sox player-manager in 1906 but committed suicide the following spring.

Garland Stahl. "Jake" Stahl is quite often mistaken as Chick's brother, which he is not. Pictured here at his first base position in a game against New York in 1903, Stahl was a good fielder but a mediocre hitter. He played one season in Boston before going to Washington for four seasons. College educated and independently wealthy, Jake played for the love of the game. He would later return to Boston.

22

The First Fall Classic, 1903. The gate at the Huntington Avenue grounds in Boston is crowded with "Royal Rooters" as the Americans prepare to take on the Pittsburgh Pirates in the first World Series. A best-of-nine post season series was planned to settle the world's baseball championship. The series opened in Boston on October 1st with a Pirates victory over Cy Young. The teams split the next two before heading to Pittsburgh.

Boston's Royal Rooters. The Huntington Avenue grounds' stands are jam packed with cranks as their Pilgrims return home on October 13, 1903, for the eighth game of the World Series. The Boston team was one win away from the championship, having overcome a three-games-to-one deficit. Bill Dineen took the mound and pitched a four-hit shutout for his third victory.

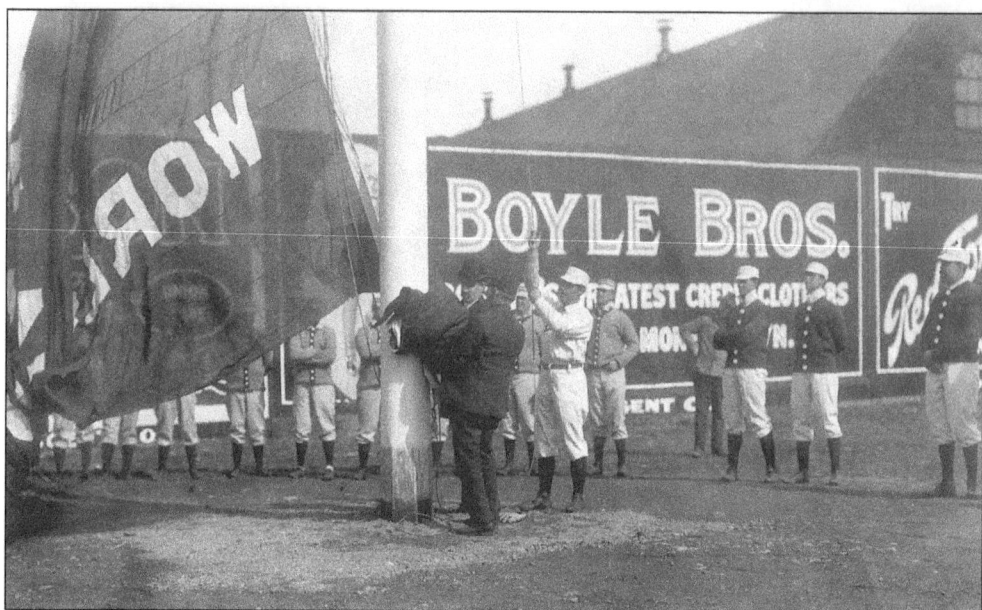

Opening Day in Boston, 1904. Captain and Manager Jimmy Collins prepares to hoist the first modern World Champions banner to fly over the Huntington Avenue Grounds. Behind third baseman Collins are right fielder Buck Freeman, who led the league in home runs with 13 and RBIs with 104; first baseman Candy LaChance; and left fielder Patsy Dougherty, tops in the league with 104 hits in 590 chances.

The Boston Dugout, 1904. Veteran catcher Lou Criger sits with two visitors to the home field. Manager Hugh Duffy (left) and Umpire Tim Hurst (right) take in early season action. Owner of the major league's highest single-season batting average (.438 in 1894), Duffy was running the Phillies club. Later, as a Red Sox coach, he would tutor a young Ted Williams. Hurst was a hard nose umpire in both leagues, often settling arguments over calls with his fists.

The Champion Among Champions. Boxing champion John L. Sullivan visits with Captain Jimmy Collins in the dugout during the spring of 1904. Sullivan, a Boston native, is well known as the bare-knuckle heavyweight boxing champion of the world. Having last fought in 1896, John L. was a well-known fixture around Boston.

A Game Face, 1906. Aptly named Fielder Jones shows himself to be a stern taskmaster at the helm of the Chicago White Sox. A veteran center fielder, Jones often suspended players for making mistakes, being out of shape, or for drinking. He is the first American League outfielder to execute an unassisted double play.

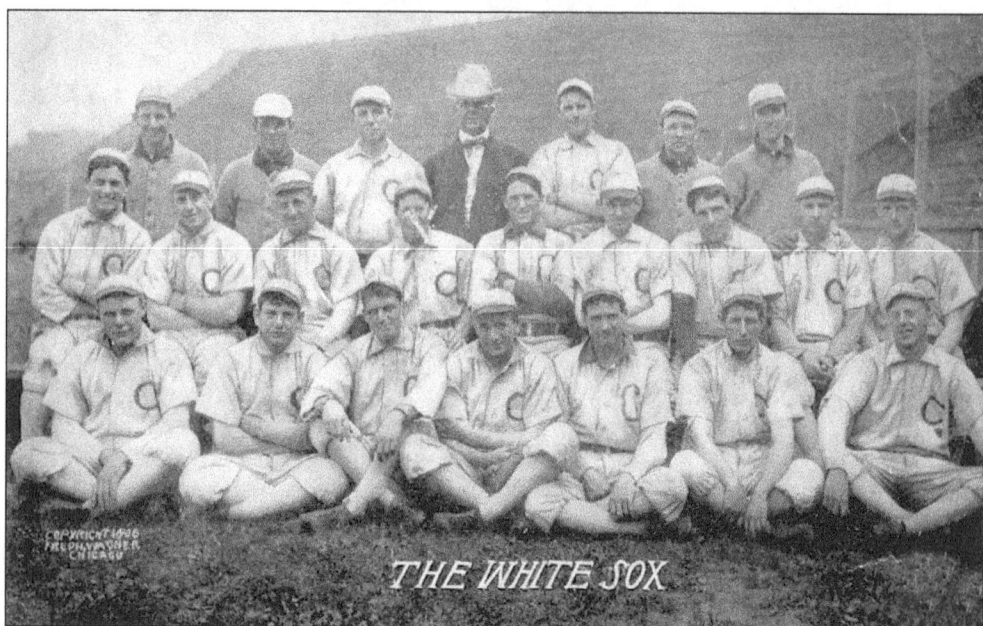

THE WHITE SOX

The "Hitless Wonders," 1906. Led by Fielder Jones, this group of lightweight hitters became the surprise AL pennant winners in 1906. Hitting a paltry .230 as a team and leading the league in walks with 255, they finished three games ahead of second-place New York. These White Sox were long on pitching and defense. The staff posted a league-high 32 shutouts with Doc White winning the ERA crown with 1.52. Center fielder Jones tied with first baseman Jiggs Donahue for fielding honors at .988.

Montford Montgomery Cross. Monte Cross, a veteran NL shortstop, was lured from the cross-town Phillies by Connie Mack to play for his Athletics. He promptly topped AL shortstops in putouts in 1902 and 1903. Finishing a strong second in 1907, the Athletics were hard put to replace Cross after he retired at the end of the season.

Two

THE TIGERS ROAR

The 1907 Detroit Tigers. Hughie Jennings (front row holding the dog) inherited a sixth place team when he signed on as manager during the early months of 1907 and transformed them into pennant winners. It would be the first of three consecutive AL pennants for the Tigers, the first time any AL team "three-peated." Jennings decided to play a brash young kid from Georgia as a regular and Ty Cobb responded with his first batting title at .350 with a league leading 116 RBIs. Sam Crawford, batting behind him at fourth in the order, finished second at .323. The pitching staff boasted three twenty-game winners: "Wild" Bill Donovan went 25-4 with a league-leading .862 percentage; Ed Killian went 25-13; and George Mullin went 20-20, posting his third straight twenty-victory campaign. Entering September, the Tigers were in a three-way race with Philadelphia and Chicago. A crucial three game series with the A's on the last weekend of the month saw the Detroit team win the first two and their first AL pennant by six percentage points.

The "Ee-Yah" Man. Hughie Jennings learned the baseball trade as the shortstop of the colorful, powerful, brawling Baltimore Orioles of the late 1890s. Ever an inspiration to his players he would occupy the coaches box, pull up fistfuls of grass and bray like a mule while dancing on one leg. He earned a law degree and built up a successful off-season practice in his native Pennsylvania.

The Georgia Peach. Purchased from the minor leagues for $750, Ty Cobb broke into the majors in 1905. Manager Jennings made him a regular outfielder in 1907 and Cobb became the youngest player to win the batting title. It was the first of 12 and the first of nine in a row, both still records. Cobb would bat over .400 three times in his career and finish with the highest lifetime batting mark, .367.

Davy "Kangaroo" Jones. Sure-handed outfielder Davy Jones came to the Tigers in 1906 and became a steadying influence in left field on the fiery Cobb and the surly Crawford. Brought over from the Cubs to replace Matty McIntyre (who could never get along with Cobb), Jones was a speedy lead-off man who batted in the high .200s consistently.

"Wahoo Sam" Crawford. Batting in the clean up spot behind Ty Cobb, the left-hand hitting Crawford began to drive in more than 100 runs a season, leading the league in RBIs three times in the 1910s. He and Cobb worked closely on the bases, pulling off some intricate double steals. When Sam came to bat, Cobb was often on third base, either hitting a triple or stealing his way around. Crawford often walked and, on a signal from Cobb, would speed up and take off for second base. At the same time, Cobb would break for home.

Opening Day, 1907. Brass bands and speeches by city officials always marked opening day in Detroit. The parades started from the players' hotels, with both teams participating and continued right into the ball yard. The ceremonial first pitch would be thrown out by a dignitary and was always caught by the old-time Detroit Wolverine catcher Charley Bennett.

Bennett Park, 1907. Colorful advertisements adorn the left field wall at Bennett Park. Davy Jones poses in the far right corner and one can see the "wildcat" stands which were illegally erected on private property. Owner Frank Navin spent years attempting to get them permanently demolished, finally buying the property and building his own grandstands.

Major League Endorsements. The center field wall at Bennett Park is adorned with paid advertisements from some of the leading manufacturers of the day. In addition to local advertisers such as P.J. Schmidt shoe store, the Detroit Taxicab Company, and Stroh's beer, national brands like Beeman's pepsin gum and the ever-present Turkish Trophy cigarettes would compete for space. The flagpole over the Stroh's sign was moved from pre–1900 Recreation Park.

William Edward Donovan. "Wild Bill" got his nickname from his tendency to wildness. He was durable and had to be, as he threw more pitches than most hurlers did. Jumping to Detroit from Brooklyn in 1903, he had his best year in 1907, when he went 25-4 and led the Tigers to their first pennant. In 1908, he went 18-7 and 8-7 the following season. His World Series results were poor, winning only one of five decisions over three years. He died tragically in a train accident in 1923.

Cy Young Day. On August 13, 1908, the AL took time out in the middle of a hot pennant race to honor one of its own. A team of all-stars traveled to Boston to play an exhibition game. Here Fielder Jones presents one of three silver loving cups to Young while Jake Stahl, Ty Cobb and others look on. Cy also received $6,000, but the Red Sox lost 3-2 on a tenth-inning triple by Jimmy Collins and a single by Jack Coombs.

Back Up Back Stop. Second string catcher Fred Payne played four seasons in the majors, two for the Bengals, relieving starter Charley Schmidt from time to time. He was involved in a controversial play early in the 1908 season. In a game against the White Sox, he stepped in front of a batter to catch a throw to the plate on an attempted suicide squeeze play. The umpire allowed the play to stand but was later overruled by Ban Johnson, thus saving the squeeze play as an offensive tool.

Hard-Charging Shortstop. Owen Joseph "Donie" Bush made his debut in mid–September 1908 and immediately stabilized an infield that was riddled with injuries. The 5-foot, 6-inch, 140-pound shortstop became a clever lead off hitter with a good batting eye. He led the league in bases-on-balls five times during a 16-year career. He and Cobb presented opponents with a strong base-stealing offense.

Wabash George Mullin. The 5-foot, 11-inch, 188-pound fastballer spent his semi-pro years in Wabash, Indiana, where he won a bride and signed two major league contracts with Brooklyn and Detroit. He picked the team closer to his new home and debuted in Detroit in 1902. He led the AL in walks each year from 1903 to 1906 but improved to league highs in percentage (.784) and wins (29) in 1909. He is a .263 lifetime hitter and was often used as a pinch-hitter.

Ed "Kickapoo" Summers. A key acquisition to the Tigers pitching staff was Ed Summers, a Logoda, Indiana native. His 24-12 record in his rookie season paced the Bengals to their second AL pennant. The tall knuckleballer started and won both games of a double-header in late September versus the Athletics, the second game a 1-0, ten-inning, two-hitter. Rheumatism hurt his pitching, sending him to the minors in 1912.

Setting the Ground Rules. The World Series of 1908 hosted a Tigers-Cubs rematch and before the start of the game in Detroit, the opposing mangers met with the umpires to discuss the ground rules. From left to right are Cubs' manager Frank Chance, NL umpire Bill Klem, AL umpire Tom Connolly, and Tigers' manager Hugh Jennings. The Tigers managed to win one game in five as both pitching and hitting disappeared. Klem and Connolly were the first umpires named to the Hall of Fame.

The Camera Never Lies. In late August 1909, Connie Mack brought his Philadelphia Athletics into town, trying to catch the league-leading Tigers. Here Ty Cobb slides hard into third base, spiking Frank Baker on the arm. The Athletics claimed that it was intentional and Ban Johnson considered a lifetime suspension for Cobb until *Detroit News* photographer Bill Kuenzel presented this photograph, which proved otherwise. Cobb slid away from Baker, who is out of the base path.

The Tall Tactician. Born Cornelius McGillicuddy, Connie Mack spent 60 years in baseball, starting as a catcher with Washington in 1886. In 1897 he managed and ran the business affairs of the Milwaukee team in Ban Johnson's Western League. After four years of learning his trade, Johnson made him an offer to organize and manage the Philadelphia team in the new AL. That began a 50-year reign in the dugout and front office as the Athletics took 6 of the first 14 pennants in the new league.

The A's in Action. Second baseman Eddie Collins bats against New York Highlander pitching during the 1909 season. Note the high crouch of New York catcher Jeff Sweeney. Collins, a Columbia University graduate, was one of the key players on Connie Mack's great teams of 1909–1914. A member of the famed $100,000 infield, Collins is considered one of the greatest second baseman in ML history.

Long Tom Hughes. A then impressive 6-foot, 1-inch right-hander, Hughes debuted with the Cubs in 1900, completing 32 starts and striking out 225. Jumping to the Red Sox the next year, he helped them to the first World Series with a 20-7 mark as the third starter behind Cy Young and Bill Dineen. Traded to Washington in 1905, Long Tom would never again win 20 games in a season and finished with a career 3.09 ERA.

The Capital Team. Right fielder Bob Ganely joined the Washington Senators in 1907 after two seasons with the Pittsburgh Pirates and became their everyday outfielder. With a total of five major league seasons, he enjoyed his best in 1907, hitting .273, scoring 73 runs, and stealing 40 bases. He also led all AL outfielders in errors that season. His hitting declined after that, ending his career in 1909.

The Ever Ready Battery. One of the best batteries in baseball teamed the Immortal Walter Johnson with Charley "Gabby" Street in 1908. Street, a Huntsville, Alabama native, became famous for catching a baseball dropped from the Washington Monument. It must have been a windy day, as he missed the first 14 tries. Nicknamed "Old Sarge" during service in World War I, he is referred to as Walter Johnson's catcher even though the two were together for just four seasons.

37

The Big Train. A 6-foot, 1-inch right-hander with long arms, Kansas-born Walter Johnson was the AL's premier pitcher although he played the whole of his career for the lowly Senators. Not an overnight success, it wasn't until his third major league season (1909) that he turned his career around and became a winning pitcher. In 21 seasons he won 416 games, amassing a record 110 shutouts and winning 38 1-0 games. With exemplary control, his walk ratio is less than 1 for every 4.1 innings—but he had wild streaks and plunked a record 206 batsmen. In the days before electronic speed guns, Johnson was believed to throw the fastest ball in the game, forcing the explanation of "you can't hit what you can't see" from more than one opponent. Johnson once had five wins in nine days, with three shutouts in 1908. His 66 wins over Detroit are the most for any AL pitcher against any one team.

Sluggers Compare Notes. Hitting legends Ty Cobb and Nap Lajoie discuss the fine art of hitting before a contest during the 1909 season. Two of the games best, the pair was often locked in a batting title struggle. In 1909, Cobb finished first and Lajoie third, but the following season saw what was probably the most hotly contested batting race ever. Lajoie finished with .384 to Cobb's .385.

Jay Austin Clarke. "Nig" Clarke was one of the first Canadian players to have an extended career in the majors. A highly rated defensive catcher, he began his career with Cleveland in 1905. He suffered with arm problems, a shortcoming that Detroit's Germany Schaefer took advantage of. In a tie game against Cleveland, Schaefer stole second, thinking the runner on third would score. Clarke refused to throw, so Germany stole first again, then stole second again, the second time drawing an errant throw allowing the winning run to score.

The Trade That Almost Was. Cleveland right fielder Elmer Flick began his ML career with the Phillies in 1898 and compiled a lifetime NL mark of .344. He jumped to the Philadelphia Athletics in 1901, following Nap Lajoie. Barred from playing in Pennsylvania, both players were sent to Cleveland. Flick won the AL batting title in 1905 with a .306 average. After the 1907 season he was considered in a trade for Ty Cobb, but it never went through.

The Trade That Was. The Philadelphia Athletics signed Joseph Jefferson Jackson in 1905, but the illiterate son of Brandon Mills, South Carolina, didn't get along with his teammates and their cruel mocking humor. Connie Mack gave up on him and shipped him off to Cleveland for Bris Lord in 1910. Accepted as he was by his Cleveland teammates, Shoeless Joe responded with the great years of his career. A natural hitter, he hit for power with yearly averages of .387, .408, and .395 with the Naps.

King of the Pitchers. Six-foot, three-inch, right-hander Addie Joss threw a one-hitter in his 1902 debut for Cleveland. The 22-year-old rookie led the AL with five shutouts that season en route to a 17-13 record. Joss used a good fastball and an extremely effective curveball to record the second best ERA in ML history of 1.88. After only nine seasons, tubercular meningitis took his life at age 29.

A Superb Second Base. An exceptionally big man to play second base, Larry Lajoie was a graceful infielder with exceptional speed and better than average hands. In 1909, he led the league in double plays with 55 and had a .953 fielding average. Lajoie managed the Cleveland team from 1905 to 1909. During that time the team was called the Naps in his honor.

Spring Training. Gathering again in Hot Springs, Arkansas, are members of the Boston Red Sox pitching staff. Among those pictured are (left to right): Ralph Glaze, George Winter, Cy Young, and Rube Kroh. Sitting in front of the group is the trainer, Charlie Green from Roxbury, Massachusetts. Standing behind Cy Young is "Nuf-Ced" McGreery, a Boston saloon keeper and ardent Red Sox fan who ended baseball arguments with "nuf-ced".

Sharing a Milk Carton. Two of baseball's finest put half a cheek each on a milk carton during warm-ups early on in their careers. They share more than a place to sit, though. Both Tris Speaker and Ty Cobb played center field and both were purchased from the Southern Leagues for the grand sum of $750.

Throwin' Smoke. Born Howard Ellsworth Wood, Smoky Joe Wood had one of the best fastballs in baseball history that compared favorably to Walter Johnson's. In fact, Johnson himself once said, "…there's no man alive can throw harder…" A rookie in 1908, Joe had the one of the best seasons a pitcher could have in 1912, when he went 34-5, completing 35 of his 38 starts.

Tristram Speaker. In his 1907 rookie year, Cy Young used to hit Tris Speaker fly balls to sharpen his ability to judge in advance distance and direction. It must have worked as his Hall of Fame plaque reads "the greatest center fielder of his day." Blessed with great speed and a powerful swing, he hit 106 triples and stole 266 bases in seven seasons for Boston. He is the all-time ML leader in outfield putouts with 6,706.

43

An Afternoon At The Ballpark. Hilltop Park in upper Manhattan features a game between the Philadelphia Athletics and the New York Highlanders during the 1908 season. One of the most exciting seasons in baseball history for both leagues, at least four AL teams were in contention through September. Typical of the Dead-Ball Era ballparks was the overflow crowd, which literally ringed the playing field. Opposing managers and the games' umpires would meet before play began and agree on the ground rules, which dealt with balls hit near or into the crowd. The National Games' growing popularity would usher in a new style of park. The steel and concrete stadium, with a much larger seating capacity, would replace the wooden fire trap accommodations and get the fans off the field and into seats.

A Princely Thief. One of the best fielding first basemen of his time, "Prince Hal" Chase repeatedly threw games for the quick money he could make betting against his own team. He led American League first basemen in errors seven times and holds the career mark with 285. On the positive side, he tied the ML mark for putouts by a first baseman in a nine-inning game with 22. His unscrupulous play eventually got him banned for life.

Lightning Strikes. Six-foot, two-inch Ray "Slim" Caldwell was once struck by lightning while pitching for the Highlanders. He recovered and finished the game, beating the Athletics 2-1. The lanky spitballer had only two decent seasons in New York, going 17-9 and 19-16 in 1914 and 1915. He was one of the pitchers allowed to use the spitball after it was banned.

A Short Stop in the Majors. As the American League entry in New York struggled to evolve and identify itself, several players had brief careers in baseball. One of these is left-hander Pete Wilson, a Springfield, Massachusetts native who spent two seasons with the Highlanders before returning to obscurity. His totals for 1908 and 1909 are 9-8 with a 3.29 ERA striking out 72 while walking 76 batters.

Take That to the Bank. William Franklin "Birdie" Cree spent several seasons as the regular left fielder for the Highlanders from 1908 through 1915, but decided that banking was a steadier occupation. The stocky right-hander had his best season in 1911, batting .348 with 30 doubles, 22 triples, and 88 RBIs.

John Milton Warhop. A stocky right-handed pitcher, Warhop had two nicknames. He was called "Chief" because his last name sounded like a "war hoop" and "Crab" because of his disposition. Never better than an average pitcher, Crab holds the Yankee season record for hit batsmen with 26. He is also famous for giving up Babe Ruth's first home run in 1915. A light hitter, he stole home twice.

Russell William Ford. Another of the few Canadians to spend considerable time in the major leagues was Russell Ford, who had a brilliant rookie season in 1910, going 26-6 with a 1.65 ERA. He followed that up with a 22-11 mark but developed chronic arm problems. He had accidentally discovered that a scuffed ball would break sharply and disguised his emery balls as spitballs, which were legal.

Determined Brownie. Catcher Nig Clarke was traded to the St. Louis Browns at the end of the 1910 season for infielder Art Griggs, who was a football star at Kansas University and the University of Pittsburgh. Clarke, a veteran catcher, was near the end of his career and the hope was to provide an experienced battery mate to control the likes of eccentric pitcher Rube Waddell.

A Stint in St. Louis. When his Athletics teammates threatened not to report in the spring of 1908 unless Connie Mack got rid of him, Rube Waddell was shipped to the Browns on February 8th for cash. The Rube posted a 19-14 record with a 1.89 ERA and in July tied the then AL single-game strikeout mark by fanning 16 of his former A's teammates. His effectiveness was slowly declining and by the end of 1910 he was in the minors.

A Premier Pinch-Hitter.
St. Louis's Dode Criss logged a total of four years in a major league uniform and led the American League in pinch hit appearances and hits in that role. The 6-foot, 2-inch, 200-pound Mississippi native played first base, outfield, and appeared as a pitcher in 30 games. He recorded 43 strikeouts in 1909 and had a win-loss record of 3-9.

Overcoming Adversity. St. Louis outfielder Danny Hoffman gets set to bat against the Highlanders during the 1908 season. Considered a top prospect for the Philadelphia A's in 1904, he was hit in the eye by a pitch from Boston's Jesse Tannehill and never recovered enough vision to stand in against left-handed pitching. He led the AL in stolen bases with 46 in 1905 and ended his nine year career with a .256 batting average.

Handsome Harry Howell. Harry Howell went 13-8 in his second year for the 1899 Baltimore Orioles team and became the workhorse for the St. Louis Browns in 1904 after brief stints with the AL Baltimore and New York teams. He averaged over 300 innings and 15 wins a season through 1908 with an ERA of 1.98 or less in three of those years.

An Ex-Spider. Bobby Wallace opened his career as a pitcher for the 1894 Cleveland Spiders. He won ten games and threw two shutouts in 1896 but moved over to third base in 1897. In 1902, the St. Louis Browns lured him away from the NL Cardinals with a five-year, no-trade $32,000 contract, which was considered a fortune at that time. He spent the next 15 seasons with the Browns and often led the league in one fielding category or another at shortstop.

All-Around Player. Roy A. Hartzell, born in Golden, Colorado, broke into major league baseball with the St. Louis Browns in 1906 as the third baseman. He was soon moving around the infield and in 1907 started working the outfield as well. His 595 at-bats led the AL in 1909 and he managed a .271 average. Traded to New York in 1911, he had a career high of .296 and 91 RBIs—the most for a Yankee in the team's first 13 years.

A Veteran Backstop. On December 12, 1908, Lou Criger was traded to the St. Louis Browns from the Boston Red Sox for catcher Tubby Spencer. Always a light hitter, Criger lasted 16 seasons in the majors because of his ability to handle pitchers. He caught every inning of the eight games of the first World Series for Boston in 1903, spurning gamblers' bribes to throw the games.

The Versatile Delahanty. Jim Delahanty was one of seven brothers from Cleveland, Ohio, five of whom played major league baseball. Big brother Ed is perhaps the best known and Jim had the next best career beginning in 1901 in the NL. He was traded from Cincinnati to Washington in 1907 and played each infield position except shortstop. He played for Detroit and hit .346 in the 1909 World Series.

Robert Alexander Unglaub. Bob Unglaub came into his own as the playing manager of the Red Sox in 1907, batting .254 with career highs 13 triples and 62 RBIs. Unglaub and pitcher Jesse Tannehill were traded to the Senators in 1908 for Casey Patten, a left-handed pitcher. Bob played three seasons for the hapless Washington team before calling it quits after the 1910 season.

Jesse Tannehill. A native of Kentucky, Tannehill was an outstanding pitcher and switch-hitting outfielder for the Pittsburgh Pirates from 1897 to 1903 when he jumped to the New York Highlanders after a salary dispute. He won 20 or more games 6 times in his 15 year career and no-hit the White Sox in 1904 as a Boston Pilgrim. Finishing his career in Washington, he played more games in the outfield than he pitched.

Hard-Charging Shortstop. After coming to the Tigers in late 1908, Donie Bush became the permanent shortstop for the next 12 seasons. In his first fall season, he led the league in assists with 567 and also in errors with 71. He would top the league in assists three more times. At the plate he amassed 1158 walks and stole 403 career bases.

A Word For The Men in Blue. Looking dapper in civilian clothes are (left to right): Billy Evans, "Silk" O'Loughlin (AL), Bill Klem, and James Johnstone (NL), respected members of the umpire corps. Evans was one of the foremost umpires in baseball history, refined, and fastidious. O'Loughlin holds the umpire's record for calling the most no-hitters with seven. Klem is regarded as the greatest of them all and pioneered the inside chest protector. Johnstone umpired in three different major leagues.

Foremost Adversaries. Ty Cobb and Honus Wagner shake hands prior to the start of the 1909 World Series. Both appear to be smiling, which soon after the first pitch was thrown, undoubtedly stopped. This would be Cobb's third and last World Series appearance. The 1909 classic is the first World Series to go seven games, with Pittsburgh's Babe Adams winning all three of his starts.

Three

THE ATHLETICS DOMINATE

The $100,000 Infield Plus One. From left to right are Stuffy McInnis, Danny Murphy, Frank Baker, Jack Barry, and Eddie Collins. When Collins became a regular in 1909, Murphy became the odd man out and was bumped to right field. This infield was together for four years and their total batting average was .319. Danny Murphy, exiled to the outfield, hit .323 over the same period. Connie Mack had built what would appear to be the perfect team and come closer than any other AL team to dominate the circuit throughout the Dead-Ball Era. They won six pennants and three World Championships during this time period. Of the starting pitching staff, two would end up in the Hall of Fame; "Chief" Bender and Eddie Plank were rotated with Jack Coombs and Harry Krause. After an unusual third-place finish in 1912, the team rebounded to win their last two pennants as a team.

The Mastermind. Connie Mack sits in the Athletics dugout and plans strategy during the 1910 season. Mack, one of the few managers to not wear a uniform on the job, never went out on the field. He would wave players into position with his scorecard. He liked tall, strong pitchers and considered pitching to be 75% of the game.

Charles Albert Bender. Born of a German father and a Chippewa mother, "Chief" Bender accepted his Native American identity but signed autographs "Charley Bender." He began a 12-year Athletics pitching career in 1903, going 17-15; by 1905, he was pitching shutout ball in the World Series. He was just hitting his stride in 1909, posting an 18-8 record, when everything jelled for the A's.

Ira Thomas. A huge catcher at 6-feet, 2-inches, 200-pounds, Thomas was one of Connie Mack's favorites, who picked him up for cash from the Detroit Tigers in 1908. He played on four championship A's teams, but only in 1911 did he catch over 100 games. He shared catching duties with Jack Lapp.

Harry "Jasper" Davis. A native Philadelphian, Davis began his career in 1895 with the New York Giants. With Pittsburgh in 1897, he walloped a league leading 28 triples. Signing on with the 1901 A's, Davis continued his slugging ways and led the AL in home runs from 1904 through 1907. He also led in doubles in 1902, '05, and '07 and was the RBI leader in '05 and '06. He was named the A's first captain and managed in Connie Mack's absence.

Jack Barry. At the heart of the $100,000 infield stood shortstop John Joseph Barry, signed in 1908 off the campus of Holy Cross. He spent most of his 11-year-career with Philadelphia and was considered vital to the team's success. Barry was a reliable fielder and led AL shortstops in double plays in 1912. By 1910, his batting had improved to .259 with 60 RBIs and the next season he had a career high 30 steals.

Hal Krause. Harry William Krause, a San Francisco native, set the league on fire as a rookie in 1909, winning his first ten starts. Six of those ten victories were shutouts and four of those were won by a 1-0 score. Krause finished the season with an AL leading ERA of 1.39 and an 18-8 record. His 1909 ERA is a record low for American League rookies.

Platoon Catcher. Philadelphia A's backup catcher Jack Lapp broke in with the team in 1908. He platooned as a backstop with Ira Thomas for the next eight years and played on four pennant winners (1910–11, 1913–14). His best season was in 1911, when he led all AL catchers with a .353 batting average in 68 games. Jack died of pneumonia at age 35.

John Franklin Baker. Frank "Home Run" Baker was a powerful slugger, a native Maryland farm boy coming to the A's in 1908 and holding down the hot corner in the $100,000 infield. In his first full season, Baker led the AL third basemen in putouts and assists, in putouts in 1910, double plays in 1912, in putouts again in 1913 and '14.

Ralph Orlando Seybold. Connie Mack brought "Socks" Seybold with him from the Western League when he formed the A's in 1901. In 1902, Seybold hit a record 16 home runs that lasted until Babe Ruth shattered it in 1919. He was consistently among the AL leaders in home runs making him one of the few true sluggers in the dead ball era. An injury ended his career in 1908.

Ossee Schreckengost. Schreck, as he was commonly referred to, teamed up with Rube Waddell to form an outstanding battery for the early Athletics. Connie Mack regarded him highly as a defensive catcher and handler of pitchers. Schreck wouldn't sign a contract one year until Waddell stopped eating crackers in bed (they roomed together). Mack wrote it into the Rube's contract and he stuck to it.

"Colby Jack" Coombs. Not because he was "cheesy," but because he was signed off the campus of Colby College in Maine did Jack gain his moniker. On September 1, 1906, he pitched 24 innings to set an AL record. His opponent, Boston's Joe Harris, is the only one who shares that distinction. In 1910, Coombs threw 13 shutouts (an AL record) among his 31 wins that season.

Another Rube. Rueben Oldring was acquired from New York for cash in October of 1905 and played the 1906 season as a back-up infielder for the A's. He moved to the outfield in 1907, where he became a fixture for the next 11 seasons. Oldring had career-high numbers in 1910, batting .307 with 14 triples and 57 RBIs.

The "Cocky" College Kid. The premier player in Connie Mack's $100,000 infield was Edward Trowbridge Collins, the former captain of Columbia University's baseball team. Nicknamed "Cocky" because of his confidence and not his attitude, Collins was active as a player for 25 seasons, 20 of those as a regular. He never won a batting title because he played during the same time as Ty Cobb, but he has a .333 lifetime average with 3,311 hits (eighth all-time).

A Special Presentation. Second baseman Eddie Collins is presented with a brand new car as members of the A's and the Boston Braves look on. This award was made prior to the start of the 1914 World Series, as those two teams were squared off together. The "Miracle Braves" took less than two months to go from last place to first in the second half of the season.

In the Outfield. So much is said about the $100,000 infield that the outfield is often overlooked. Here, from left to right, are Bris Lord, the "Human Eyeball;" Rube Oldring; and Danny Murphy; who roamed the outfield for the champion A's. Lord was signed off the sandlots in 1905 and was reacquired from Cleveland in an even-up trade for "Shoeless" Joe Jackson, in time for the championship run.

Can't Wait For Spring. Opening Day in Detroit in 1911 finds playing conditions just a little rough. Davy Jones leads off against the Chicago White Sox in nearly "white-out" circumstances. Owner Frank Navin always argued with AL President Ban Johnson for a later start to the season, but never won. Billy Sullivan Sr. handles the catching duties.

Fair Play in the Fall Classic. New York Giants manager John McGraw shakes hands with Philadelphia A's slugger Harry Davis as umpire Tom Connolly looks on before the 1911 World Series. This was the long awaited rematch from 1905, when the Giants defeated the A's 4 games to 1 and every game was a shutout. McGraw had his team wear the same black uniforms as a taunt.

Opening Batteries. Three quarters of the starting batteries for Game 2 in Philadelphia are caught by the camera. From left to right are Ira Thomas, Eddie Plank, and Giants catcher Chief Meyers. Missing is Giants' pitcher Rube Marquard, with a 24-7 regular season record. With three Giants' errors and a Baker home run, the A's tied the series at one game apiece.

Gettysburg Eddie. After being sidelined with a sore arm and not pitching at all in 1910, Eddie Plank came back and posted a 23-8 record for 1911. A hard-luck World Series pitcher, he started and won Game 2 and came on in the tenth inning of Game 5 and lost, giving up a sacrifice fly to Fred Merkle.

The "Chief" Workhorse. Chief Bender had three starts in the 1911 World Series, squaring off against the incomparable Christy Mathewson in games one and four. He lost a 2-1 decision in Game 1 while striking out 11 and defeated "Big Six" in Game 4. Bender went the distance in the sixth and deciding game, giving up only two runs in a 13-2 pasting.

Action at the Polo Grounds. Giants pitcher Christy Mathewson hits the dirt as catcher Meyers fails to stop Eddie Collins from stealing second base in the fourth inning of Game 3 on October 17th in New York. Frank Baker homered in the top of the ninth to send the game into extra innings. The A's scored twice in the eleventh inning and won by a 3-2 score.

Game 6 Action at Shibe Park. Over 20,000 screaming cranks packed Shibe Park on October 26th to see if the A's would prevail. Here it is, the third inning, and Ira Thomas crosses the plate on Bris Lord's double, off Giants pitcher Red Ames, tying the game at a run apiece. Rube Oldring is the next man up as the A's mascot is there to offer congratulations.

The Origin of Home Run Baker. Frank Baker watches another one that's "long gone!" Home runs were still a rarity in 1911, as games were played for one run at a time. Baker paced the AL with 11 dingers that season, but earned his nickname that October. In Game 2, with Eddie Collins on, Baker got hold of an inside fastball and sent it out. The clout held up as the A's won 3-1. Baker drilled a Mathewson pitch deep to tie up Game 3 in the ninth and the nickname stuck.

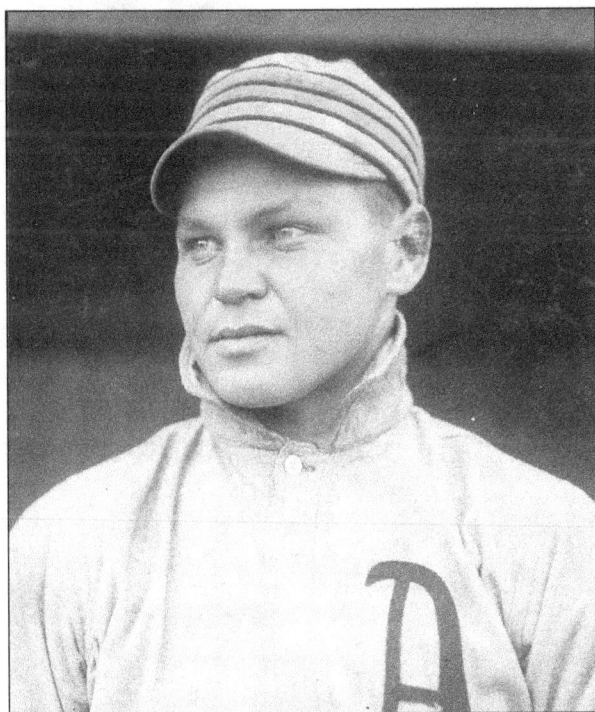

A Chance To Play. Just before the 1910 World Series was about to begin, A's center fielder Rube Oldring broke his leg. Amos Strunk hit .278 in a losing effort, but became the regular center fielder for the next nine seasons in Philadelphia. He became highly regarded for his defensive skills and topped AL outfielders in fielding average five times. No slouch at the plate, he was a solid left-handed hitter who rarely struck out.

The Old Fox. Clark Griffith earned his nickname as a right-handed pitcher for Cap Anson's Chicago Colts in 1893. He used six different pitches in his repertoire, including a screwball and a quick-pitch delivery. But it is as a manager that he is most often remembered. First directing the White Sox, then the Highlanders, he found his home in Washington in 1912. He revolutionized baseball with his reliance on the bullpen and his use of relief pitchers.

A Hapless Right-Hander. Bob Groom began his major league career on a dubious note. From June through September 1909, the Washington rookie set a major league record by losing 19 games in a row. He finished the season at 7-26, tying the AL mark for losses. Groom also led the league in walks with 105 but managed to find success in 1912 by going 24-13.

Germany Schaefer. Traded with Red Killifer in mid–1909 from Detroit for Jim Delahanty, Schaefer had a career-high season for Washington, hitting .334 in 1911. One of the most colorful characters in baseball history, he once wore a raincoat out to his position to convince the umpire to call a rainout. After 1911, he spent most of his time on the coaching lines.

Clyde "Deerfoot" Milan. Clark Griffith claimed that Milan was the best center fielder the Senators ever had. He played shallow and used his incredible speed to catch up with long fly balls. Signed on the same scouting trip as Walter Johnson, Milan was no slouch on the base paths. In 1912, he broke Ty Cobb's single season stolen base record with 88 and had 495 steals lifetime.

69

William "Dolly" Gray. An Ishpeming, Michigan native, Dolly was nicknamed for a popular Spanish-American War ballad, *"Goodbye, Dolly Gray."* This luckless left-hander lasted three seasons, compiling a 15-51 record for the cellar-dwelling Senators. Poor Gray lost a one-hitter when after a two-out error, he walked seven straight batters.

Conroy and Killifer. "Wid" Conroy and Red "Lollypop" Killifer pose for a photograph during the 1910 season. Conroy, near the end of his playing career, was the regular third baseman, while Killifer played every infield position during his seven year career. Out of the playing ranks by 1917, "Lollypop" had a long and successful career managing in the Pacific Coast League.

A Battery Reunited. Lou Criger caught most of Cy Young's 511 career victories. The battery began in 1896 in Cleveland and St. Louis in the National League and Boston in the American League until Criger's trade to the Browns in late 1908. Cy Young's winning percentage was .620, even playing for some poor teams and he topped 30 victories five times.

Collins Miffs One. Eddie Collins lets one get through him, since no one plays perfectly all the time. Collins led AL second basemen in errors in 1912 with 38 and usually averaged 20 or so per season. Even so they played exceptional defense, yet Connie Mack dismantled his $100,000 infield in 1915, selling Collins to the Chicago White Sox.

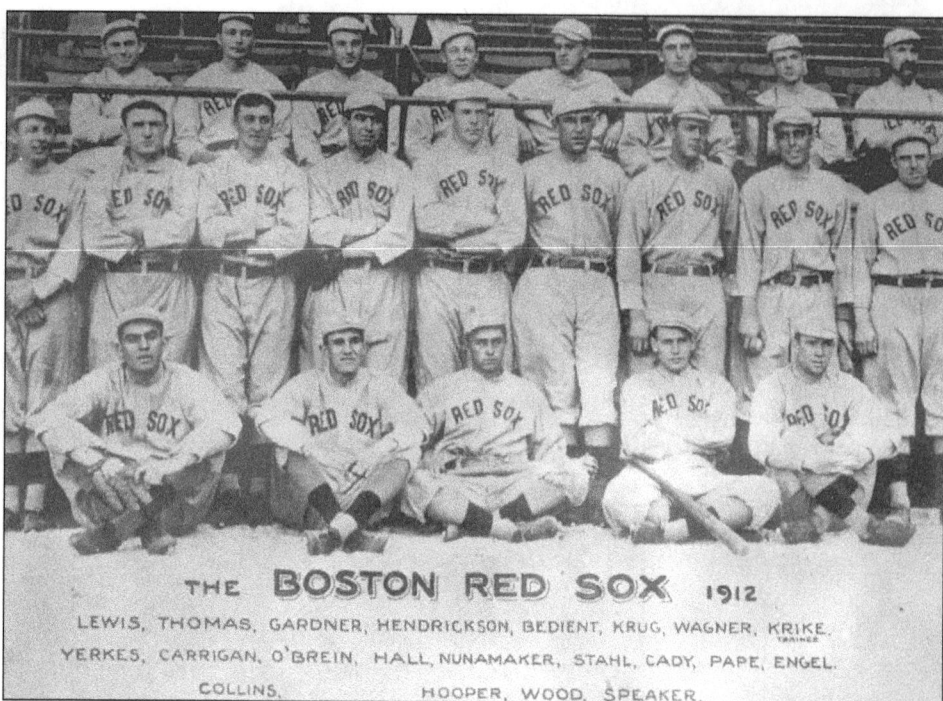

THE **BOSTON RED SOX** 1912

LEWIS, THOMAS, GARDNER, HENDRICKSON, BEDIENT, KRUG, WAGNER, KRIKE.
TRAINER
YERKES, CARRIGAN, O'BREIN, HALL, NUNAMAKER, STAHL, CADY, PAPE, ENGEL.
COLLINS. HOOPER, WOOD, SPEAKER.

The Pilgrims Win a Flag. Winning back-to-back pennants in 1903 and 1904, the Boston team was rebuilt over the rest of the decade and won a pennant in 1912 when the A's finished a surprising third. The group won 105 games behind the spectacular pitching of Smoky Joe Wood, who notched 16 straight victories, en route to a 34-5 finish. The team batted .277, with Tris Speaker tying for the league lead in home runs with 10.

The Second Time Around. Player-manager Jake Stahl has his second try at managing in 1912 after taking the Senators to two seventh-place finishes in 1905 and 1906. The veteran first baseman hit .301 with 60 RBIs, while guiding the team to a first-place finish, 14 games ahead of the Washington Senators. He would be dismissed half-way through the next season.

72

Eddie Cicotte. A native Detroiter, Eddie Cicotte was picked up by Boston for the 1908 season and went 11-12 in his first full campaign. He enjoyed his best year in Boston in 1909 with an ERA of 1.97 and a 13-5 record. Still learning his trade, he would develop quite an arsenal of deceptive pitches and pinpoint control. He was sold to the White Sox in 1912.

A Hard-Hitting Outfield. From left to right stand Harry Hooper, Tris Speaker, and Duffy Lewis, the heart of the Boston offense. Known as the Million Dollar Outfield, the trio had 455 assists with Hooper's strong arm in right accounting for 150 of them. Tris Speaker and Duffy Lewis figured in most offensive categories in 1912.

George Edward Lewis. "Duffy" Lewis began his major league career with Boston in 1910 and hit .283 with 8 home runs. He became so adept at playing his position in left field in the brand new Fenway Park in 1912, that the incline at the base of the big green monster became known as "Duffy's Cliff." In the championship season, he had a personal high of 109 RBIs.

A Career Season. Twenty-two-year-old Smoky Joe Wood enjoyed a spectacular season in 1912, posting a career high 34-5 record, league highs in wins, winning percentage (.872), complete games (35), and shutouts (10). Joe recorded 258 strikeouts while surrendering only 82 walks in 344 innings pitched. He also batted .290 and hit one home run.

Ernest Grady Shore. This 6-foot, 4-inch right-hander's baseball career is closely mixed with Babe Ruth's. Ernie spent a brief time with the New York Giants in 1912 and came up to Boston from Baltimore together with Ruth. He spent four winning seasons in Beantown, posting a 19-8, 1.64 ERA record in 1915. In 1917, when Ruth was ejected after walking the first batter, Shore relieved, picked off the runner and pitched a perfect game.

Bill "Rough" Carrigan. After Jake Stahl was dismissed as manager, platoon catcher Carrigan took over the dissent-riddled team. He brought the team home second in 1914 and after Babe Ruth was added to the pitching staff, led Boston to AL pennants and World Championships in 1915 and 1916. Carrigan quit at the pinnacle of his success to become a banker in his home state of Maine.

Playing the Sun Field. Harry Hooper nearly became a civil engineer before signing a big bonus contract with Boston in 1909. He taught himself to play the difficult sun field in right and invented the rump slide to snag short flies. He was the Red Sox lead off hitter for 18 seasons and claimed that he was the one who convinced manager Ed Barrow to move Babe Ruth to the outfield on the days when he wasn't pitching.

At The Hot Corner. Third baseman Larry Gardner rockets one out in practice in Boston. He was rock-solid at third from 1912 through 1917, after signing with the Red Sox from the University of Vermont in 1908. An above-average left-handed batter, it was his sacrifice fly in the tenth inning of Game 7 that did in the New York Giants in the World Series of 1912.

Liked By Cobb. Left fielder Duffy Lewis was one of the few players that Ty Cobb supposedly liked. Yet Lewis's fondest memories were of throwing Cobb out attempting to stretch hits at Fenway. Lewis was a noted line-drive hitter and a good RBI man. He became the first major league player to pinch hit for Babe Ruth, when he was a rookie pitcher.

BOSTON-AMERICAN LEAGUE CHAMPIONS—1912

1912

O'BRIEN P. / CARRIGAN C. / WOOD P. / NUNAMAKER C. / SPEAKER C.F. / HENRIKSON R.F. / HALL P. / CICOTTE P. / GARDNER 3d B. / WAGNER S.S. / THOMAS C. / HOOPER R.F. / LEWIS L.F. / HAGERMAN P. / LEONARD P. / Dr. QUIRK / PAPE P. / ENGLE U / YERKES 2d B. / BRADLEY 1st B. / KRUG S.S. / BEDIENT P. / BUSHELMAN P. / CADY C. / McCARTHY Mascot / STAHL 1st B.

World Champions. A team lineup superimposed over a brand new Fenway Park in Boston proclaims the capture of the 1912 AL pennant. Everyone has their picture taken, including McCarthy (mascot, second from right) and team physician Dr. Quirk (in bowler hat). Heinie Wagner served as captain and had career highs that season of .274, 68 RBIs, and 75 runs scored.

Wahoo Sam Crawford. For 19 major league seasons, Sam Crawford patrolled the outfield, first for the Cincinnati Reds and, starting in 1903, for the Detroit Tigers. His fielding percentages were always in the high .900s and only once did his errors reach double digits. He is most famous for hitting triples, 312 of them, the most ever. But what is largely forgotten is his long-ball power. Crawford has 97 career home runs and when he retired in 1917, held the AL career record with 70. Sam was the big fish in the Bengal dugout when Ty Cobb showed up in 1905. Although they never got along, they played well together both offensively and defensively. In Crawford's words Ty Cobb "... sure wasn't easy to get along with." Long after their playing days, Cobb would campaign to get Sam elected to the Hall of Fame. Both Tiger players would find no World Series success—both were failures at bat in 1907, 1908, and 1909.

White Sox Outfield. From left to right are Shano Collins (RF), Ping Bodie (CF), and Ray Demmitt (LF), the sinister looking outfield for Chicago. By 1913, Collins was one of the AL's top defensive outfielders. Ping Bodie was born Francesco Stephano Pezzullo. He took Bodie from the California town in which he once lived and Ping from the sound of the ball off his bat. Ray Demmitt was a regular in only three major league seasons.

Master Strategist. Connie Mack checks his ever-present scorecard for notes on the opposition as Ira Thomas and Stuffy McInnes follow the action. McInnes replaced Harry Davis at first base in 1911 and stayed on for three pennant winners. A right-handed pull hitter, he could also punch the ball to the opposite field. He batted over .300 from 1910 to 1915.

"Chauncey" Dubuc. Jean Joseph Dubuc started in the major leagues with Cincinnati in 1908 fresh off a college campus. He developed into an above average pitcher in the American League, twice winning 17 games for the Detroit Tigers. Dubuc also hit two home runs in 1913 and in 1919, once again in the NL, won six games in relief. His career ended in scandal—his association with Sleepy Bill Burns got him banned for life in 1920.

Bennett Park From the Grandstand. Bennett Park action from the grandstand behind home plate. New York Yankee pitcher Ray Caldwell winds up to pitch to Detroit's Sam Crawford. Moments earlier, Ty Cobb swiped home plate out from under catcher Ed Sweeney who holds the Yankee record for stolen bases for a catcher in a season (19).

Four

TIGERS, NAPS, NATS, AND BROWNIES

A Hard Hitting Outfield. From left to right are Davy Jones, Ty Cobb, and Sam Crawford. With a changing left fielder, the Tiger outfield pair of Ty Cobb and Sam Crawford played together from 1905 to 1917 and usually wound up finishing first and second in the batting race. In 1905, Matty McIntyre was the regular left fielder. He hated Cobb so much that Hugh Jennings moved Crawford from right to center as a buffer. Davy Jones was next and a settling influence on Cobb and Crawford. Then came Bobby Veach in 1913, a left hand hitting left fielder who stayed for 11 years and batted .306 or better for 8 of those years. In 1919, he led the league in hits, doubles, and triples but finished second to Cobb, hitting .355 to Cobb's .384. When Sam Crawford retired in 1917, Harry Heilmann took his place. A Cobb protégé with the bat, Heilmann would chase him for many a batting title.

One Honey of a Trophy. The George "Honey Boy" Evans Trophy was given to the major league batting champion from about 1909 until his death in 1915. Evans was a music composer and a great baseball fan. This is the trophy for 1912, which was won by Ty Cobb, who topped all hitters with a .410 batting average. Cobb won this trophy in 1909, 1910, 1911, and 1912.

"Deerfoot" Milan. Washington Senators' center fielder Clyde Milan strikes a pose with what appears to be one of the largest Dead-Ball-Era gloves around. The fleet-footed Milan stole 83 bases in 1913 and behind the pitching of Walter Johnson, who posted a 36-7 mark with a 1.09 ERA, the usually cellar-dwelling Nationals finished a surprising second, six and one-half games behind the Philadelphia A's.

Always Ready. A veteran of eight major league seasons, William "Birdee" Cree stands ready to go to work, bat in hand and his glove hooked to his belt. His lifetime average of .292 with 332 RBIs and 97 stolen bases and three seasons as the regular left fielder were not enough—he quit baseball and went into banking.

The Yankee Backstop. Edward Francis "Jeff" Sweeney was the regular catcher for the New York team, doing the bulk of the duty from 1910 through 1914. A fair shooter, he reportedly didn't like the way Hal Chase was mocking manager Frank Chance for the team's amusement in 1913, so he told Chance. Chase was suddenly dealt to Chicago. Sweeney swiped 19 bases in 1914—the most ever by a Yankee catcher.

The Spitball Master. Charles "Heinie" Berger played two seasons with the American Association in which he won 20 games both times and came up with Cleveland in 1907. The stocky right-hander twice won 13 games for Cleveland, in 1908 and 1909, and established the club record for right-handers with 162 strikeouts.

Bill Wambsganss. Born William Adolph and nicknamed "Wamby," he played most of his 17 seasons for Cleveland. Initially a utility infielder, he settled in as the regular second baseman by 1917 and could handle the glove well. He is most known for his unassisted triple play in the 1920 World Series—the only one so far.

Back In Cleveland. Cy Young was traded to the Cleveland Naps team for two players and $12,500 on February 18, 1909. The aging veteran would play two seasons in Ohio and post a 26-25 record. After pitching 11 games for the Boston Braves in the NL in 1911, he retired. After a career 511-313 record, he had put on weight and was no longer able to field his position. Without a twinge of pain in his arm, Cy Young retired.

Sylveanus Augustus Gragg. Vean Gragg, a powerful left handed pitcher, had a superlative rookie season with Cleveland in 1911, going 23-7 and led the American League with a .767 winning percentage and an ERA of 1.81. He followed that up with two consecutive 20-13 seasons, then suffered arm trouble, which reduced his efficiency. He was traded to Boston in mid–1914, but never enjoyed the same success.

The "Kid" at Second. Eddie "Kid" Foster, at 5-feet, 6-inches, was considered the best hit and run man in the business. After a short season with New York in 1910, he was up to stay in 1912 with Washington, playing third base regularly. He led the league in at-bats in three of the next four seasons, and averaged 50 or more RBIs.

John Wesley Coombs. After handling the pitching chores for Connie Mack's Philadelphia Athletics from 1906 to 1914, Jack Coombs was dealt to the Brooklyn Dodgers, when Mack dismantled his champions after losing to the Boston "Miracle" Braves. Coombs remained unbeaten in World Series competition and won more for the 1916 Brooklyn team. After retirement, Colby Jack went on to become a championship coach with Duke University.

Choose Your Weapon. Tiger immortal Ty Cobb would often swing three bats while waiting his turn at bat. Often berated for this supposed show of strength, Cobb never let on that once up to the plate, the bat felt lighter, making the swing faster. Always the one to gain any advantage, Cobb has the highest lifetime batting average—.367.

The Protégé. Harry "Slug" Heilmann joined the Detroit Tigers in 1914 and was up to stay in 1916. The 6-foot, 1-inch, 200-pound right-handed slugger played the outfield with Cobb and maybe took some batting tips from the Hall of Famer. Hitting in the high .200s, he would have a breakthrough season in 1919, hitting .320 with 95 RBIs.

Player, Umpire, Manager. George Moriarity spent his first two seasons of what would ultimately be a 50-year baseball career with the Chicago Cubs as a utility player. After three seasons with the Yankees, he went to Detroit and took over third base duties from the retiring Bill Coughlin. A good fielder with an average bat, George was strongest in base running, accumulating 248 lifetime steals. Best known as an AL umpire for 22 years, he took time off to manage the Tigers (1927–28).

A Man In Blue. Jack Sheridan began umpiring in the 1890 Players League and continued on in the National League until 1897. In 1901, he started a 13-year career with the AL and was soon known for his consistency and fairness. He would use old hotel register books as inside chest protectors, enabling him to crouch down behind the catcher in order to get a closer look at pitches. Jack called the first AL forfeit in 1901, in a game between Detroit and Baltimore.

The "Joss Game" All-Stars. On Friday, April 14, 1911, the baseball world was stunned by the news that Addie Joss, star pitcher for Cleveland, had died. The 31-year-old had succumbed to meningitis, an inflammation of the membranes surrounding the brain. Charles Somers, the owner of the Cleveland team, wanted to put together a benefit game for the Joss family. These games were a long-standing tradition in baseball, but Somers was calling for the greatest benefit ever seen, with some of the greatest players. On Monday, July 24th, they gathered to play and raised well over $13,000 for Lillian Joss. They are: back row (left to right): Bobby Wallace, Frank Baker, Joe Wood, Walter Johnson, Hal Chase, Clyde Milan, Russ Ford, Eddie Collins. Front row: Germany Schaefer, Tris Speaker, Sam Crawford, Jimmy McAleer, Ty Cobb, (his trunk got lost), Gabby Street, and Paddy Livingston.

Top row: Bush, McInnis, Barry, Collins, Baker, Mgr. Mack, Oldring, Thomas

Middle Row: Daley, Schang, Lapp, Brown, Bender, Wyckoff, Davis, Orr. *Bottom Row:* Houck, E. Murphy, Plank, Strunk, Bailey, D. Murphy, Walsh, Taff

1913 PHILADELPHIA FATIMA TURKISH BLEND CIGARETTES AMERICANS

The Philadelphia Athletics. American League champions in 1913, Connie Mack's team was in the middle of its dynastic run. They won the AL flag by six games with consistent pitching from five starters who also earned 11 saves between them. "Home Run" Baker led the league in home runs with 12 and in RBIs with 126. At least one A's batter finished in the top five in every offensive category.

Top row: Martin, Trainer Henry Harper Boehling Gandil Johnson McBride Engle Gideon Gallia

Second Row: Hughes, Schaefer, Morgan, Manager Griffith, Milan, Shanks, Moeller, Groom. *Sitting:* Mullin, Calvo, Foster, Altrock, Ainsmith, Laporte, Acosta, Williams

1913 WASHINGTON FATIMA TURKISH BLEND CIGARETTES AMERICANS

The Washington Senators. Usually last in the American League, the Senators finished as high as second twice during the Dead Ball Era—1912 and 1913. Led by Walter Johnson's 1.39 ERA, they posted a 91-61 record while Boston ran away with the flag. In 1914, the "Big Train" went 36-7 with a 1.09 ERA to lead the league. They were just outpaced by the powerful Athletics.

90

The Cleveland Indians. An American League charter franchise, the Indians acquired their new nickname in 1915 when they also acquired Tris Speaker from Boston, giving up Sam Jones, Fred Thomas, and $55,000 in cash. Never placing higher than third, the team rallied to finish second twice to end the Dead Ball Era in 1918 and 1919.

The Boston Red Sox. Alternately called the Americans, Pilgrims, and Puritans, the team in Boston was quite successful during the first two decades of the American League. Pennant winners in 1903 and 1904, they spent the rest of the decade rebuilding. The Red Sox captured the 1912 AL flag, the 1912 World Series, and had back-to-back championship seasons in 1915 and 1916 with the help of a new left-handed pitcher named Babe Ruth.

Chief Bender. One of the dominant pitchers during the first two decades of AL play was Charles Albert Bender, who came into the league in 1903 and remained until 1914. He chalked up 191 victories and led the league three times in winning percentage over that time. Bender was an all-around player, appearing in several games as an infielder and outfielder and was an excellent sign stealer.

World Series Managers. Philadelphia Phillies manager Pat Moran shakes hands with Boston's Bill Carrigan before the 1915 World Series. Moran, a back-up catcher during his playing days, took the Phillies to the pennant on his first try. Carrigan took over the helm in Boston as playing manager in 1913, leading the Red Sox to the first of two consecutive World Championships.

On to Boston. Traded to Boston for $8,000 from Philadelphia in mid–1915, Jack Barry proved to be the last piece of the puzzle for the pennant. Used exclusively at second base, he hit .262 for Boston in 78 games. He had only 3 hits in 17 tries in the World Series, however, and didn't play at all in 1916. Barry replaced Bill Carrigan as manager in 1917 and finished second.

Jumpin' Joe Riggert. Utility outfielder Joe Riggert displays his vertical abilities for the camera in his sole American League season, 1911. This Janesville, Wisconsin, native got into 50 games that season and managed 13 RBIs in only 146 at-bats. He reappeared in the National League in 1914 and again in 1919 before dropping out for good.

"Tioga George Burns".
George Henry Burns began
his career with the Detroit
Tigers, appearing at first base
in 137 games. He batted
.291 with 57 RBI. He led
the American League in hits
with 178 in 1918 playing for
the Philadelphia Athletics.
Burns drove in the winning
run for Cleveland in the 1920
World Series and was traded
to Boston the following year.

Harry Bartholomew Hooper. A member
of the Boston Red Sox from 1908 to 1920,
Hooper was one-third of the million dollar
outfield. He was strongly religious and
was supposed to have prayed for a Boston
victory in the final game of the 1912 World
Series. He made a bare-handed, game-
saving catch off Larry Doyle that prevented
the Giants victory. In 1915, he became
the first player to homer twice in a single
World Series game.

Wood to the Outfield. During the spring of 1913, Smokey Joe Wood slipped on some wet grass while fielding a ground ball and broke his thumb. He was never the same and at the age of 26, Wood had to give up baseball. Intent on resuming his career, Wood persuaded Cleveland to give him another chance in 1917. He abandoned the mound in 1918 and moved to the outfield, batting .296 in 119 games. In one afternoon in New York, he hit two home runs.

Buck O'Brien. Thomas Joseph O'Brien, a Brockton, Massachusetts, native made it to the Red Sox in 1911 as a right-handed spot starter. He posted a 5-1 record and completed the five games he started, winning one in relief. In 1912, O'Brien was 20-13 for the World Champions, but lost both of his starts in the World Series.

The Winningest Left-Hander. George Herman Ruth started his career as a minor league pitcher with the Baltimore Orioles of the International League before he was sold to the Boston Red Sox in 1914. He appeared in four games his rookie season, posting a 2-1 mark. Coming into his own the next season, he soon became one of the game's hot pitchers, with seasons marks of 18-8, 23-12, 24-13, and 13-7 through 1918. His consistency helped Boston to three pennants (1915,'16,'18) and three World Championships. Ruth led the league with a 1.75 ERA and 9 shutouts in 1916 and won a career high 24 games in 1917. In World Series competition, he posted 29 consecutive scoreless innings, a record that would stand for 42 years. The Babe pitched one game in 1916 and two in the 1918 World Series, winning all three games and racking up an 0.87 ERA, third best all-time.

The Young Sultan. The Boston Red Sox could not long ignore the hitting abilities of their young southpaw, who, as a pitcher, was batting a career-record .307. His 1917 batting average of .325 (in 123 at-bats) trailed only Ty Cobb, George Sisler, and Tris Speaker. The following season, Ruth began playing in the outfield in between starts and led the American League in home runs with 11 in 1918 and a ML record 29 in 1919.

The Bambino in Red Stockings. Oftentimes considered to be the best player of all times, Babe Ruth changed the way baseball was played with his particular slugging style. He developed into the prototype of the modern superstar during his tenure as a Red Sox, before bursting onto the national stage in Yankee pinstripes in 1920.

97

Sailor Bob. Another Connie Mack giveaway, Bob Shawkey was probably the best pitcher that the New York Yankees had for eight seasons starting in 1916. New York spent $18,000 for the young right-hander and he became the team's workhorse, going 24-14 with a 2.21 ERA in 53 appearances. The strong man on a staff could always be called in relief and Bob got seven of his victories that way. He was also credited with 8 saves. In 1918, he was aboard the battleship *Arkansas* as a petty officer, where he got the nautical nickname.

In and Out of Pinstripes. George Whiteman was in and out of baseball, playing three games for Boston in 1907, 11 games as a Yankee in 1913, and was 35 years old when called up again by the Red Sox in 1918. George played the outfield when Babe Ruth was pitching and stuck around long enough to be the defensive hero of the 1918 World Series, making a superb catch in the eighth inning of the final game.

Strength Up the Middle. Roger Peckinpaugh was the premier shortstop of his day with wide range to go along with big hands. Not always graceful, he pursued the ball relentlessly and effectively. Peck came to the Yankees from Cleveland in mid–1913 and managed the team for 14 games in 1914. He was a steady batsman and had a 29 game hitting streak in 1919.

Walter Clement Pipp. Wally Pipp was acquired by the Yankees in 1915 from Detroit for the waiver price and became the regular first baseman for the next ten seasons. Wally led the American League in home runs with 12 in 1916 and 9 in 1917 and was a consistent hitter. He would play a valuable role in the Yankees rise to prominence.

"Bunny" High. Hugh "Bunny" High twists himself into a grimace in his first of three years as a regular Yankee outfielder. Unable to break into the Detroit outfield of Cobb, Crawford, and Veach, the oldest of the three High brothers found a place in New York in 1915. He fielded his position well, scoring in the high .900s.

Picking the Home Run Bat. Frank Baker sat out the 1915 season in protest over salaries and Connie Mack sold him to the Yankees in 1916 for $35,000. The veteran third baseman responded with a league high 2.8 home run percentage, tagging ten of them in 360 at-bats. Frank sat the 1920 season due to the illness, then death, of his first wife. He returned in time to help the team to its first World Championship.

Robert Hayes Veach. Bobby Veach was the Detroit Tigers' regular left fielder for 12 years, playing beside Sam Crawford and Ty Cobb. A consistent .300 hitter, he shared the AL lead in RBIs with Crawford (112) in 1915, and led in hits, doubles, and triples in 1919. He finished second to Cobb in that year's batting race.

A Superb Lead Off Man. Donie Bush squares around to bunt his way on base. A clever batsman with an excellent eye, Bush led the league in bases-on-balls for the fifth time in his career in 1914 with 112. A sure-handed shortstop, he held that position down for 13 seasons, before being traded to the Senators in 1921.

Bernie Boland. Bernard Boland came up to the Detroit Tigers in 1915 and stepped right into the starting rotation. He was a regular starter for five seasons before he broke his arm. His best season came in 1917 when he went 16-11 with a 2.65 ERA. His effectiveness nearly gone, he was traded to the Browns in 1921. He had a sharply breaking curveball and used it to strike Babe Ruth out three times in one game.

Oscar Joseph Vitt. Ossie Vitt came up to the Detroit Tigers in 1912 and in 1915 became the regular third baseman. Always a marginal ballplayer, he lasted ten years in the majors by being a smart, fiery competitor. His best season at the plate was 1917, when he hit .254 with 47 RBIs.

Cobb Ties Into One. The Georgia Peach continues his winning ways at the plate for the Detroit Tigers. Through the teens, his batting prowess continued to win him titles in 1913, '14, '15, '17, '18, and '19. After two seasons of .420 (1911) and .410 (1912), Cobb batted over .360 in each of those years.

Following the Master. Harry Heilmann, attired in Tiger pinstripes, was working as a bookkeeper when he was offered his first baseball job. "Slug" hit .305 for Portland in the Northwest League and was purchased by the Tigers for $1,500 in 1913. Up to stay in 1916, he would compete with Cobb in many batting title battles, finally getting one in 1921.

Pure Aggression. The grit of determination is plainly seen on Ty Cobb's face as he goes hard into third base in a game against New York. His reputation as a fierce competitor, one he encouraged, overshadowed his skill at the plate. Harassed continuously as a rookie in 1905, he learned to do everything he could to gain the advantage over an opponent. Cobb was a natural right-hander who taught himself to bat from the left side of the plate in order to be closer to first base. He amassed 4,191 base hits in his career along with 892 stolen bases. Branch Rickey once said, "Cobb lived off the field as though he wished to live forever. He lived on the field as though it was his last day." He was possessed.

A New Sheriff in Town. Del "Sheriff" Gainor was acquired for the waiver price by Boston after a four-year career in Detroit in 1914 to give the Red Sox some depth at first base. The 6-foot West Virginian hit a pinch-hit single in the fourteenth inning in Game 2 of the 1916 World Series, ending the longest game in World Series history and preserving Babe Ruth's first post-season pitching victory.

The Senior Sullivan. Ty Cobb called Billy Sullivan Sr. the best catcher "ever to wear shoe leather." From 1901 to 1912, with Billy calling the pitches, the White Sox won two pennants, came within two games of two others, and never finished lower than fourth place. His superior defensive skills kept him in the game for 16 years, as his .212 lifetime batting average is the second worst of all time among those with 3,000 at-bats.

Edward Augustine Walsh. "Big Ed" Walsh, an ex-coal miner from Pennsylvania, was drafted by Chicago's Charles Comisky who acted on a tip given to him by the Red Sox in 1904. Ed learned how to throw the spitter and became one of the game's dominant pitchers. In 1908, he threw 464 innings en route to an unbeatable 40-15 record. No major league pitcher has ever won as many since.

George Daniel Weaver. "Buck" Weaver made his debut with the Chicago White Sox in 1912 as the regular shortstop. He topped the league in errors at that position with 71 and again in 1913 with 70, but he also had 392 putouts and 520 assists to compensate. Weaver hit .300 in 1917 and in the World Series played all six games and batted .333.

Five

BLACK SOX, YANKEES, AND A FLAG FOR CLEVELAND

Spitball Artists. From left to right are Ed Walsh, Jim Scott, Eddie Cicotte, Joe Benz, "Reb" Russell, Bill Lathrop, Red Faber, and one of the team trainers. "Big Ed" Walsh was suffering from growing arm problems, but "Death Valley Jim" Scott was hailed as an Ed Walsh, Mordecai Brown, and Cy Young all rolled into one. Relying on a spitter and a screwball, the 235-pound right-hander led the AL in starts with 38 in 1913, going 20-20. Eddie Cicotte, just traded to the Sox in 1913, had pinpoint control. Another good spitter and knuckleball ace was Joe "Butcher Boy" Benz, who one-hit Walter Johnson once in 1914. Ewell "Reb" Russell was a rookie sensation in 1913 with a 22-16 record. Bill Lathrop appeared in a total of 25 games over two seasons in Chicago, while Red Faber saved his career in 1911 by acquiring the spitter.

Sure Handed at Short. Lewis Everett "Deacon" Scott led all American League shortstops in fielding average for eight consecutive seasons from 1916 to 1923. He also played in 1,307 straight games, a record that Lou Gehrig would eventually smash to bits. He took over in Boston in 1914 and later in New York, playing in five World Series for the two teams.

Hubert Benjamin Leonard. "Hub" Leonard was a superb left-hander in the days of Red Sox greatness, but never achieved a 20-win season. He came closest in 1914, going 19-5, while recording the lowest ERA ever in major league history with a 1.01 mark. He has two World Series victories, one each in 1915 and '16 with a 1.00 ERA.

Grover Cleveland Lowdermilk. "Slim" Lowdermilk came over to the St. Louis Browns from the National League in 1915. At 6-feet, 4-inches and lean, with long fingers, he was compared to Walter Johnson, but with one exception—he couldn't control his blazing fastball. After moving from St. Louis to Detroit and then to Cleveland, he was back with the Browns in 1917 before moving once again, this time to Chicago.

The Greatest Brown of Them All. "Gorgeous George" Sisler became one of the finest first baseman in baseball history. A graduate of the University of Michigan, George started out as a left-handed pitcher, but his bat was too good not to play everyday. In his second season, he was moved permanently to first base in 1916, and hit .305. George would stay in the limelight throughout the 1920s.

Sad Sam Jones. "Horsewhips Sam" was traded to the Boston Red Sox from Cleveland for none other than Tris Speaker in 1916. He broke into the starting rotation in 1918 and posted a 16-5 record with a 2.25 ERA. For the next 22 seasons he would pitch well in the American League. He earned his "Horsewhips" nickname because of his sharp curve and the "Sad Sam" moniker because he always looked so downcast on the mound.

The Squire of Kennett Square. Herb Pennock, a native of Kennett Square, Pennsylvania, had a background as an expert rider and a master of hounds. He found his true talent on the pitcher's mound and developed into a smart, graceful, and stylish hurler. Pennock was waived by Connie Mack to the Red Sox after the World Series loss to the Braves in 1914, where he developed into a tested pitcher.

Urban Clarence Faber. The nickname "Red" would be a blessing for Urban Clarence who was a steady, even-tempered, right-handed spitballer. He began his career in 1914 and stayed with Chicago for 20 years. Faber was the pitching star of the 1917 World Series, posting a 3-1 record. He was in the Navy for most of 1918 and on the bench with a recurring arm problem and the flu during the 1919 scandalous Series.

The Twirling Dentist. Guy Harris White earned his nickname because of his degree in dental surgery from Georgetown. "Doc" White jumped to Chicago from the Philadelphia Phillies in 1903 after a season on 20 losses. In September 1904, he threw five straight shutouts. The string was finally broken when he pitched both ends of a doubleheader. Needless to say, he was an exceptional control pitcher and also a violinist, balladeer, and songwriter.

Sold to the Sox. When Connie Mack dismantled a team, no one was spared. He sold Eddie Collins to the Chicago White Sox for $50,000 in 1915. Collins responded by leading the league in walks with 118 and batted .332. He was the star of the 1917 World Series, hitting .409 with one double and nine singles in 22 at-bats. In 1918, Eddie joined the U.S. Marine Corps, but was back on a pennant winner in 1919. He was deemed one of the "honest players," was unforgiving of the eight who had sold out, but still considered the team one of the greatest he ever played on. Collins continued to play excellent baseball season after season, both in the field and at the plate. He batted over .300 year after year, and after the Dead Ball Era gave way to the livelier one, Eddie Collins kept right on going.

"The Swede is a Hard Guy." Joe Jackson made that claim after Swede Risberg threatened to kill him if he talked during the Black Sox trial. Risberg was a hard-nosed character, an average shortstop with a powerful arm, and a hatred for Eddie Collins, his double play partner. Banned for life for throwing the 1919 Series, he also fixed games in his rookie year and in 1920.

The Ringleader. Charles Arnold "Chick" Gandil ran away form home at age 17 to play baseball in Arizona. He also did some prize fighting, earning $150 per bout. Chick was sold to the Washington Senators in mid–1910, where he stayed playing first base until 1916. He made the acquaintance of Sport Sullivan, a bookie and gambler. Sullivan had rich friends and the link with the ballplayers was made to throw the Series. Gandil rejoined the White Sox in 1917 and batted a paltry .233 in the tainted 1919 Series.

A Cracker Catcher. Ray "Cracker" Schalk is credited with being the first catcher to backup plays at first and third base. He was one of the premier catchers of his day, catching a major league record four no-hitters in his career. He was the leader in several defensive categories, season after season. However, Ray was merely an adequate batter. His best at the plate came in the 1919 Series, when he batted .304.

"Happy" Felsch. Oscar Felsch broke in with the Chicago White Sox in 1915 and batted .248 in 121 ball games. He was an excellent center fielder with great range and a strong arm, still sharing the records for most double plays by an outfielder in a season with 15 and assists in a game with 4. He was just emerging as a power hitter when the scandal broke and he was banned from baseball.

114

"Fast" Eddie. Eddie Cicotte—had he not agreed to throw the 1919 World Series—would probably have been remembered as one of the game's greatest pitchers. Coming to Chicago from Boston in mid–1912, Eddie came into his own. In 1917, he led the league with 28 wins and an ERA of 1.53. He led again in 1919 with a 29-7 mark and a 1.82 ERA. Cicotte was paid $10,000 to "beat himself."

Unknowing Manager. William "Kid" Gleason is known today as the betrayed manager of the Black Sox, but he was a star player of the 1890s. He started as a pitcher for the Philadelphia Phillies in 1888 and, in 1890, notched a record of 38-17 with a 2.63 ERA. Gleason lost his effectiveness when the pitching distance was increased in 1894, so he switched to second base and played with the Orioles and Giants before jumping to the AL in 1901.

The Shoeless Wonder. Joe Jackson was traded to the White Sox from Cleveland in 1915 for three nobodies and $31,500 cash. The slugging star didn't hit as well in Chicago but still sat as the star of the powerhouse Comisky team. Joe hit .351 with 96 RBIs for the 1919 pennant winners. He had one of his best seasons the following year, slugging 12 home runs and 121 RBIs, with a .391 batting average. He could run, hit, and throw with the best of them in both leagues, but he lacked judgment, education, and common sense. Being unable to read and write put this Southerner at a distinct disadvantage. Totally out of place in the big city, Joe probably did accept the promise of $5,000 to fix the games. If he chose to ignore the promises, his .375 World Series batting average was not enough to exonerate him. It was a pure tragedy of baseball and the American way of life.

Never Snitch Weaver. Buck Weaver had one of his best series at the plate at the same time most of his teammates were deliberately having their worst. Weaver hit .324, banging out 4 doubles, a triple, and 11 singles in 34 at-bats. But he had knowledge of the fix and his "never snitch" ethics resulted in his being banned for life. He hit a career high .333 in 1920.

The Obvious Throw. Claude Preston "Lefty" Williams pitched briefly for the Detroit Tigers in 1913 and 1914. He came up to the Chicago White Sox in 1916 and turned in two fine seasons, posting records of 13-7 and 17-8 before working in a shipyard during World War I. Rooming with "Shoeless" Joe Jackson, Williams went 23-11 before the 1919 World Series. He made catcher Ray Schalk so angry, he almost charged the mound, going 0-3, with a 6.61 ERA. Williams was banned in 1920.

At His Best. Catcher Ray Schalk handled strong pitching staffs, including the 1920 White Sox starting rotation that had four 20-game winners on it. He was a workhorse, catching a hundred or more games in twelve seasons. Schalk led the league catchers in fielding and putouts eight times, four times in double plays, and twice in assists. He was at his best batting during the 1919 World Series, with a .304 average.

An Honest Starter. Richard "Dickey" Kerr was in his rookie season in 1919 and finished with a 13-7 record when the World Series loomed. Kerr won both of his starts, one by shutout, while his corrupt, star hurlers were busy losing theirs. Kerr was 21-9 in 1920 and turned in a 19-17 record in 1921. Denied a $500 raise by Sox owner Comisky, he decided to pitch for independent teams. Kerr was a successful minor league manager and converted Stan Musial from a pitcher to an outfielder.

He Could Do It With His Eyes Closed.
The "Mighty Mite" was a first-rate second baseman for the Cincinnati Reds and St. Louis Cardinals before retiring to the bench in 1917. Miller Huggins was fast and sure-handed in the field, leading the league in putouts, assists, double plays, and fielding. He was a smart, switch-hitting lead off man who chalked up 1,002 career walks and stole 50 bases a year.

Muddy Ruel. Harold Dominic Ruel had a brief stint with the St. Louis Browns in 1915 and came back up to stay with the Yankees in 1917. Ruel started out as a star catcher, was an assistant to a baseball commissioner, and a manager of the St. Louis Browns. He had a law degree and was admitted to practice before the Supreme Court.

Looking Good in Pinstripes. "Home Run" Baker watches one go as the viewer gets to see his graceful follow through. Baker had 96 career home runs, three of them in 25 World Series contests. Those dingers came against Rube Marquard and Christy Mathewson. As a manager in the Eastern Shore League, he discovered Jimmy Foxx.

To Follow Ruth. Pitcher Ernie Shore's career was intertwined with the Babe's. They ended up going to the Yankees together form Boston, with Ernie serving in a different kind of uniform in 1918. When he got back to the Yankees, he roomed with the Babe. Shore lost some of his effectiveness after his military service and retired soon after.

The Man in the Green Suit. Francis Joseph "Lefty" O'Doul was called the man in the green suit by New Yorkers exploiting his Irish sounding name. He spent most of his career in the Pacific Coast League and came up to the Yankees as a sore-armed left-hander in 1919. He saw little action in pinstripes for the next four years. His later success would be as a National League outfielder.

A Stern Taskmaster. Miller Huggins tried to buy the St. Louis Cardinals in 1917, being a shrewd investor in the stock market and was businessman enough to try. His bid was turned down and he resigned as manager. American League President Ban Johnson convinced Jacob Ruppert, principal owner of the Yankees, to pick him up. In 1918, Hug began to develop the great slugging Yankee teams that sounded the death knoll for the Dead Ball Era, by ending their carousing and bad acting.

An Historic Headache. Wally Pipp was the Yankees solid, sure-handed first baseman as the team geared up for its run at dominance of the American League. He was a major contributor to their first three pennants in the early 1920s, but in 1925, asked for a day off because of a headache that was worsened by a beaning during practice. Lou Gehrig took his place.

The Babe and His Wife. Babe Ruth stands proudly next to his wife in a New York uniform for the start of the 1919 season. Boston Red Sox owner Harry Frazee sold Ruth for $100,000—twice the highest amount ever paid for a player—in order to bankroll his Broadway shows. He also got a $300,000 loan and Boston fans got railroaded. Ruth took to his new digs, hitting .376 and blasting 54 home runs.

All-Around Brilliance. University of Michigan star George Sisler signed a professional baseball contract in 1911, while underage and without parental consent. After four years of argument and waffling, the National Commission ruled the contract invalid and made him a free agent. To Pittsburgh's loss, George signed with the Browns, like Babe Ruth, as a pitcher. His bat could not be ignored, however, and he was moved to first base even though two of his five decisions were victories over Walter Johnson. Sisler led the AL seven times in assists and three times in double plays. His 1920 statistics are among the best ever produced. He played every inning of every game and batted .407 with 49 doubles, 18 triples, and 19 home runs for 399 total bases. George went hitless in only 23 games, drove in 122 runs, and stole 42 bases. His 257 hits conclude the best single-season mark ever.

Poised To Leave the Cellar. "First in war, first in peace, and last in the American League" is an old, slightly inflated adage used to describe the Washington Senators. Except for two second-place finishes in 1912 and 1913, the Nats—as they were sometimes called—finished last four times in their first nine seasons. The improvement can be attributed to two events: the ascendancy of Walter Johnson as the AL's premier pitcher, and the hiring of Clark Griffith as manager in 1912. Griffith pioneered the use of relief pitchers and the signing of talented Caribbean players. He also acquired first baseman Chick Gandil, who played a respectable position before succumbing to fast money. Clark Griffith bought the team in 1920 and continued to lay the foundation for a winning enterprise. The Senators would be a better team throughout the decade of the 1920s and would finish in first twice.

The Deadly Submariner. Carl Mays was used mostly as a relief pitcher in his rookie season with Boston in 1915. He led the AL with five wins in relief and seven saves. Mays became an effective starter in 1917, recording a 22-9 mark followed with a 21-13 record. After winning a pair of World Series games in 1918, he demanded a trade and was dealt to New York. He had a fast rising submarine ball that on August 19, 1920, hit Cleveland's Ray Chapman in the head, killing him.

Ray Chapman. This popular Indian infielder began his major league career in 1912 and became the regular shortstop the following season. Coming into his own, he led the team in stolen bases four times and set the team record with 52 in 1917. He led the AL in runs scored and walks in 1918 and was hitting .303 with 97 runs scored when he died. Chapman liked to crowd the plate and seemed to freeze when Carl Mays delivered the fatal pitch, striking him in the temple.

A Timely Hero. George Burns came over to the Cleveland team in mid-season 1920, in time enough to play in 44 regular season games. Burns drove in the winning run in Game 7 of the 1920 World Series, to give the championship crown to Cleveland. The Indians reciprocated by trading him to Boston in 1921.

The "Hawk" at League Park. Cleveland manager Tris Speaker finagled Connie Mack into including Charlie Jamieson in an already lopsided trade in 1919. A left-handed pitcher turned outfielder, "Hawk" took wing at just the right time. From 1920 to 1931, he owned left field at Cleveland's League Park, turning in dazzling outfield plays and nine full seasons batting over .300.

Hall of Fame Fill In. When Ray Chapman's replacement, Harry Lunte, was hurt on Labor Day, Little Joe Sewell was called up in the middle of the American League pennant race. He was equal to the task, hitting .329 and helping Cleveland to its first-ever pennant. Thus began a 14-year Hall of Fame career.

The Gray Eagle Triumphs. Boston Red Sox President Joe Lannin proposed a salary cut to Tris Speaker after the 1915 World Series victory because of his falling batting average (down to a mere .322). Speaker wouldn't sign, so Lannin traded him to Cleveland. For the next eleven years he averaged .354 and in 1920, after the fatal beaning of Ray Chapman, he rallied his team on to win the pennant and World Series.

A Legend in Pinstripes. As the National Game was rocked by the revelation in 1920 of the 1919 World Series fix, the future of the game was definitely in jeopardy. The American people lost all confidence in the sport and steps would have to be taken to save it. The emergence of Babe Ruth and his style of play would serve as the saving agent. Changing the game from a strategic, scientific contest to the more dramatic offensive style kept the sport from oblivion. In 1920, Ruth smashed 54 home runs and turned in a slugging average of .847, an average no one has yet matched, to help make the game the national sport it is. The long ball spelled the end of the Dead Ball Era and ushered in the lively one.

Visit us at
arcadiapublishing.com